C.S.I.
TRAIL OF BLOOD

Darlene Stille

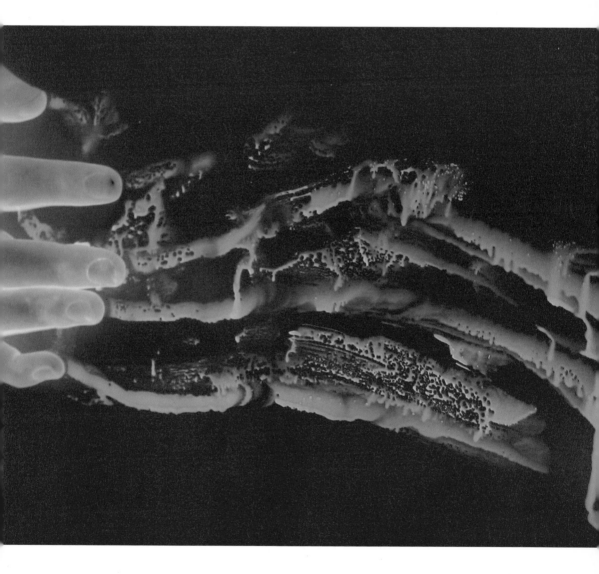

🌱 Crabtree Publishing Company

www.crabtreebooks.com

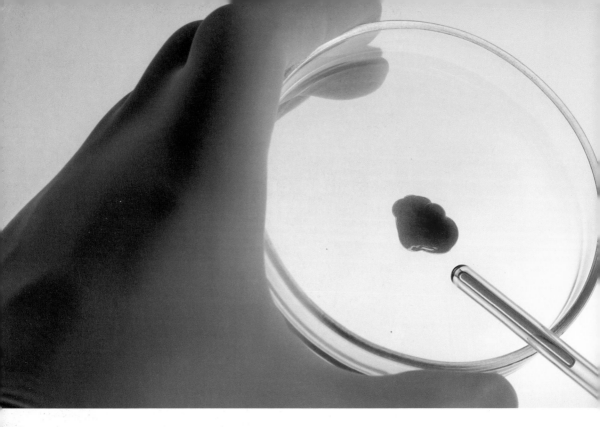

Crabtree Publishing Company

www.crabtreebooks.com   1-800-387-7650

Copyright © **2009 CRABTREE PUBLISHING COMPANY**.
All rights reserved. No part of this publication may be reproduced,
stored in a retrieval system or be transmitted in any form or by
any means, electronic, mechanical, photocopying, recording, or
otherwise, without the prior written permission of Crabtree
Publishing Company.

**Published
in Canada
Crabtree Publishing**
616 Welland Ave.
St. Catharines, ON
L2M 5V6

**Published in the
United States
Crabtree Publishing**
PMB16A
350 Fifth Ave., Suite 3308
New York, NY   10118

Content development by Shakespeare Squared
www.ShakespeareSquared.com
First published in Great Britain in 2008 by ticktock Media Ltd,
2 Orchard Business Centre, North Farm Road,
Tunbridge Wells, Kent, TN2 3XF
Copyright © ticktock Entertainment Ltd 2008

Author: Darlene Stille
Project editor: Ruth Owen
Project designer: Sara Greasley
Photo research: Lizzie Knowles
Proofreaders: Crystal Sikkens,
   Robert Walker
Production coordinator:
   Katherine Kantor
Prepress technicians:
   Katherine Kantor, Ken Wright

With thanks to series editors
Honor Head and Jean
Coppendale, and consultant
John Cassella, Principal
Lecturer in Forensic Science,
Staffordshire University, UK

Thank you to Lorraine
Petersen and the
members of nasen

Picture credits:
Alamy: Pablo Paul: p. 8 (top), 10 (bottom)
Photolibrary: Photodisc: cover
Science Photo Library: BioPhoto Associate: p. 17; Mauro
   Fermariello: p. 7; Philippe Psaila: p. 9; Revy, ISM: p. 19;
   Alexis Rosenfeld: p. 24–25; Volker Steger, Peter Arnold Inc.:
   p. 10 (top); Andrew Syred: p. 16 (bottom); Tek Image: p. 8
   (bottom), 22–23; Geoff Tompkinson: p. 21; Jim Varney: p. 13
Shutterstock: cover (background), p. 1, 2–3, 4, 5, 6, 11, 12,
   14–15, 16 (top), 18, 20, 26–27 (bottom), 28, 29, 31
Hayley Terry: p. 27 (top)

Every effort has been made to trace copyright holders, and we apologize in
advance for any omissions. We would be pleased to insert the appropriate
acknowledgments in any subsequent edition of this publication.

Library and Archives Canada Cataloguing in Publication

Stille, Darlene R.
      Forensic evidence : blood / Darlene Stille.

(Crabtree contact)
Includes index.
ISBN 978-0-7787-3815-2 (bound).--ISBN 978-0-7787-3837-4 (pbk.)

      1. Criminal investigation--Juvenile literature. 2. Blood--
Juvenile literature. 3. Forensic sciences--Juvenile literature. 4.
Evidence, Criminal--Juvenile literature. I. Title. II. Series.

HV8077.5.B56S75 2008   j363.25'62   C2008-903497-X

Library of Congress Cataloging-in-Publication Data

Stille, Darlene R.
   Forensic evidence : blood / Darlene Stille.
      p. cm. -- (Crabtree contact)
   Includes index.
   ISBN-13: 978-0-7787-3837-4 (pbk. : alk. paper)
   ISBN-10: 0-7787-3837-X (pbk. : alk. paper)
   ISBN-13: 978-0-7787-3815-2 (reinforced library binding : alk. paper)
   ISBN-10: 0-7787-3815-9 (reinforced library binding : alk. paper)
   1. Criminal investigation--Juvenile literature. 2. Evidence, Criminal--
Juvenile literature. 3. Blood--Juvenile literature. I. Title. II. Series.

   HV8073.8.S85 2009
   363.25'62--dc22

                                                           2008023540

Contents

CHAPTER 1

A MYSTERY

23-year-old man has gone missing.
e was last seen two weeks ago at work.

ere is no sign of a break-in or fight
his apartment. His clothes, suitcase,
d passport are in the apartment.

ll the rooms are very clean.
ere are no towels or tissues in the bathroom.

e apartment looks too clean.

Could it be a **crime scene**?

The police think a crime has been committed.
They have two **suspects**.

| Suspect A | Missing man |

Suspect A is the man's ex-girlfriend.
They argued before he went missing.

Suspect B

Suspect B is the man's
roommate. The police
find out the roommate
owes the man thousands
of dollars. The roommate
cannot be found.

CHAPTER 2

AT THE CRIME SCENE

The police want to find out if a crime has been committed.

The police put crime scene tape around the man's home. They send for the **crime scene investigators**. They are known as CSIs.

CSIs look for **evidence** at a crime scene. They look for evidence such as blood, fingerprints, and hairs.

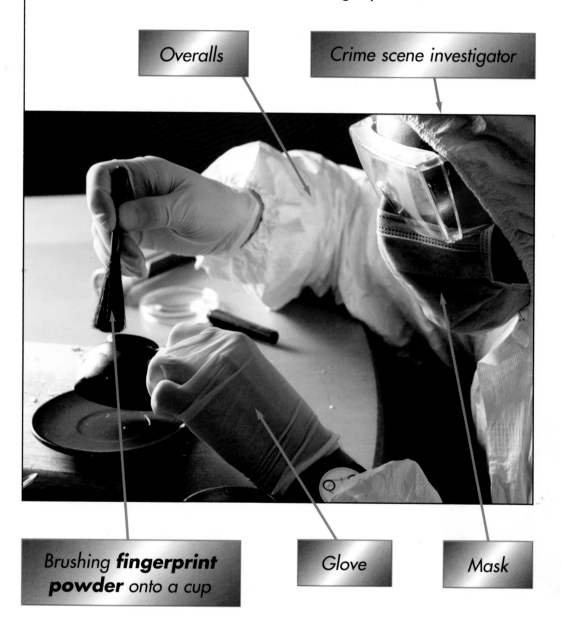

Overalls

Crime scene investigator

Brushing **fingerprint powder** onto a cup

Glove

Mask

The CSIs wear gloves, masks, shoe covers, and white overalls. The overalls and gloves prevent the CSIs from leaving their own hairs or fingerprints at the crime scene. They must keep any evidence clean.

The crime scene investigators search the entire apartment.

They take photographs and make videos.
They put markers where they find evidence.

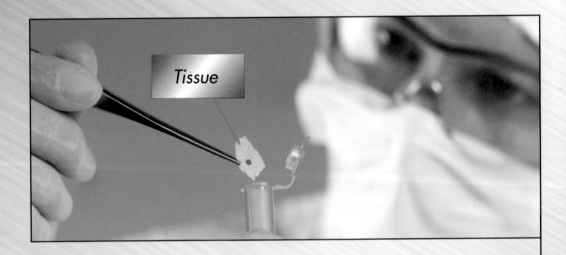

A CSI finds a tiny piece of tissue. It looks
as if there is dried blood on the tissue.

The CSI does a chemical test on the piece of tissue.
The test will show if there is dried blood on the tissue.

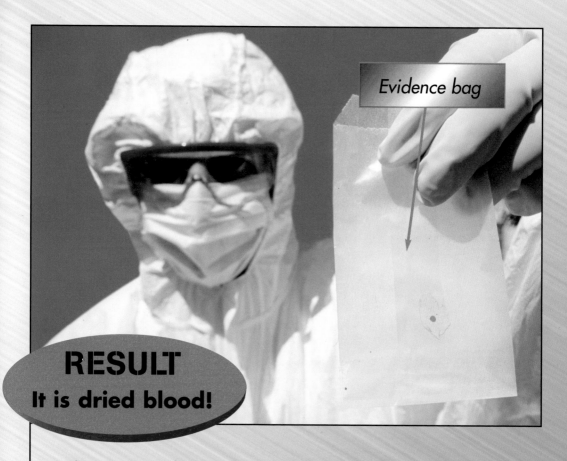

Evidence bag

RESULT
It is dried blood!

The piece of tissue is put into an evidence bag.
Then it is taken to the **crime lab**.

NEED-TO-KNOW

Blood starts to dry after three to five minutes. Wet blood
is better than dried blood for testing. Wet blood can
show if the person was taking drugs or drinking alcohol.

CSIs can collect blood from a crime scene in different ways.

They can use tape to pick up bits of dried blood.

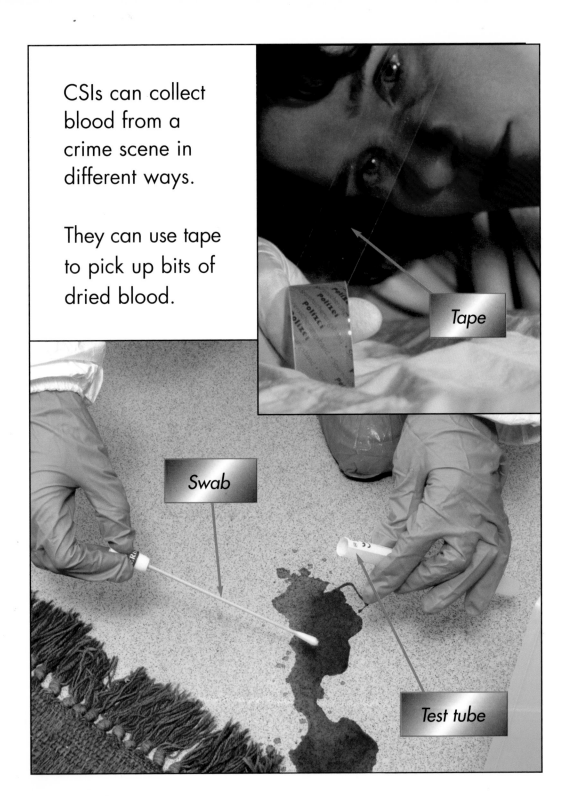

Tape

Swab

Test tube

CSIs can collect wet blood with a **swab**. Then they seal the swab in a **test tube**.

When a person is injured, blood from his or her wounds makes patterns or spatters.

The height of a blood spatter on a wall can tell scientists the position of a wound. For example, the height of the splatter can show if the **victim** was wounded on the chest or on the knee. It can also tell the scientist if the victim was standing or sitting when attacked.

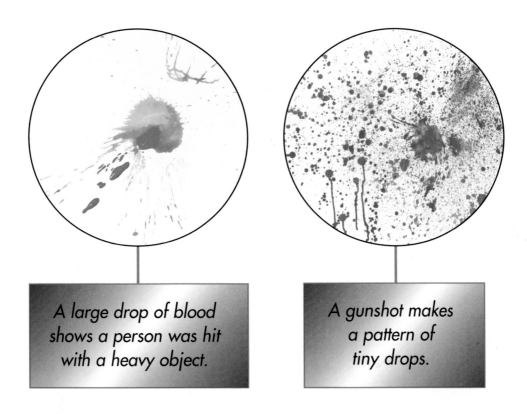

A large drop of blood shows a person was hit with a heavy object.

A gunshot makes a pattern of tiny drops.

Scientists can tell what sort of weapon caused a wound by looking at the size of the blood drops.

Scientists study the shape of the drops made by a gunshot to find out the angle of the bullet.

The CSIs search the missing man's apartment. They cannot find bloodstains or blood spatters in any rooms.

Has the crime scene been cleaned?

It does not matter how well a criminal scrubs a crime scene, the CSIs can find hidden bloodstains.

The bathtub looks very clean. But is it?

The CSIs rub a swab over an area of the bathtub to see if there are any hidden traces of blood.

Next, the swab is dabbed onto a piece of damp filter paper. Special chemicals are sprayed on the filter paper.

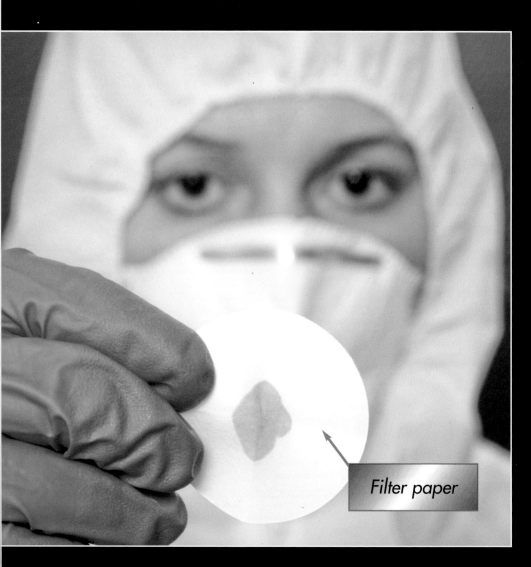

Filter paper

The filter paper turns purple. This means there is blood on the bathtub. The filter paper is taken to the lab for more testing.

The CSIs find hidden blood in the hallway, too!

Was the man stabbed in his bathroom?

Was his body dragged from the apartment?

Has there been a murder?

CHAPTER 3

AT THE CRIME LAB

The piece of tissue and the filter paper are taken to the crime lab.

Forensic scientist

A forensic scientist **analyzes** the two blood samples.

The forensic scientist tests the blood to find out if it is from a man or a woman.

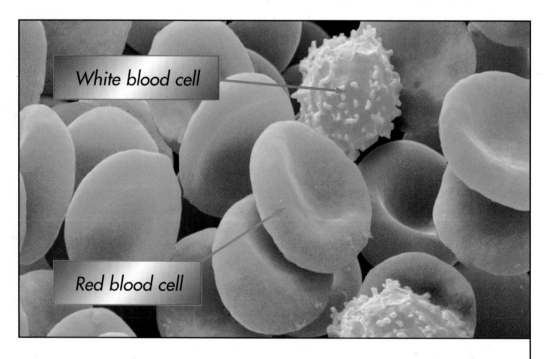

White blood cell

Red blood cell

Blood is made up of **cells**. Each white cell has a part called a **nucleus**.

A human nucleus contains two **chromosomes**.
There are X and Y chromosomes.

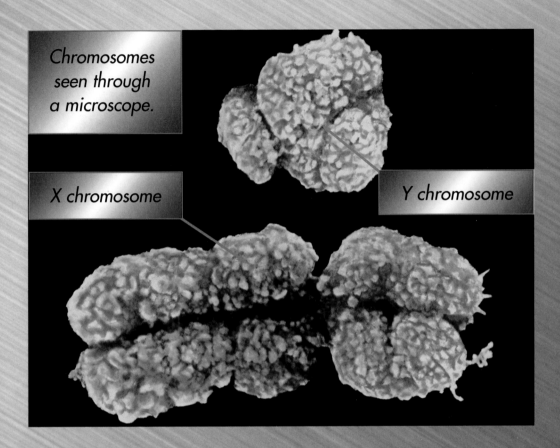

Chromosomes seen through a microscope.

X chromosome

Y chromosome

Two X chromosomes
mean the blood is
from a female.

X + **X** = female

An X and a Y
chromosome means the
blood is from a male.

X + **X** = male

RESULT

**Both blood samples
from the crime scene
are male.**

Next, the forensic scientist tests the blood to find out what blood type it is.

There are four different types of human blood.

The types are A, B, AB, and O.

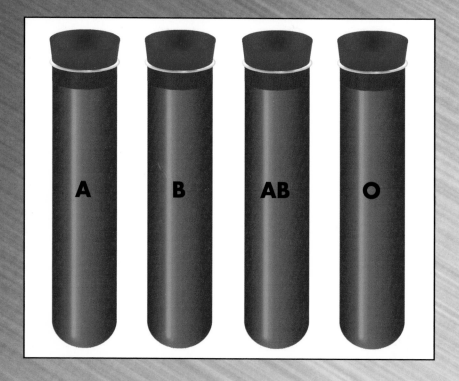

All humans are one of these four blood types.

The forensic scientist uses chemicals to test the two blood samples from the crime scene.

Different blood types react in different ways to the chemicals.

Chemicals

Each blood sample from the crime scene is mixed with three chemicals.

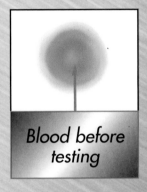
Blood before testing

B

Type B blood reacts to the three chemicals like this.

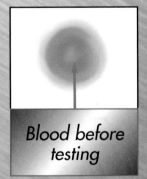
Blood before testing

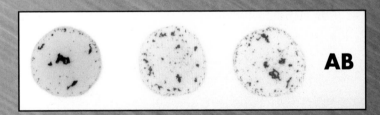
AB

Type AB blood reacts to the three chemicals like this.

RESULT
One blood sample is type B and one sample is type AB.

Forensic scientists can also check blood samples for another important clue — **DNA**.

Cells in our body are unique. They contain unique information called DNA.

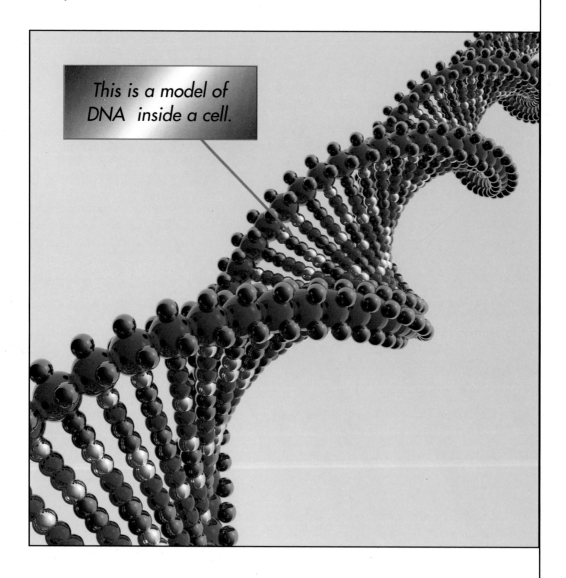

This is a model of DNA inside a cell.

Except for identical twins, no two people have the same DNA.

DNA tests are done on the two blood samples from the crime scene.

A special machine "reads" the DNA. The machine displays the information in a pattern called a DNA profile.

DNA profile

A DNA profile is unique. The police can match it to a profile from a suspect or from a victim.

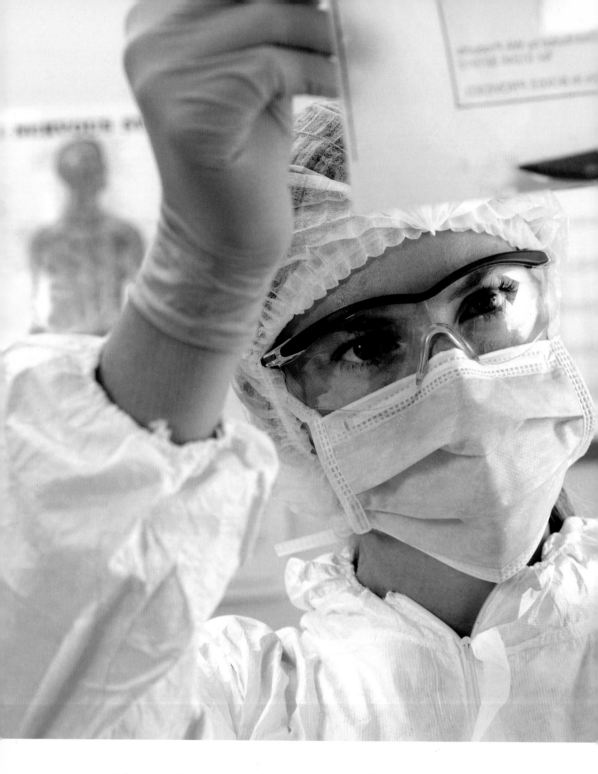

The police search the ex-girlfriend's house.
In the garden, they find a bloody knife.

The forensic scientist finds two different
samples of blood on the knife.

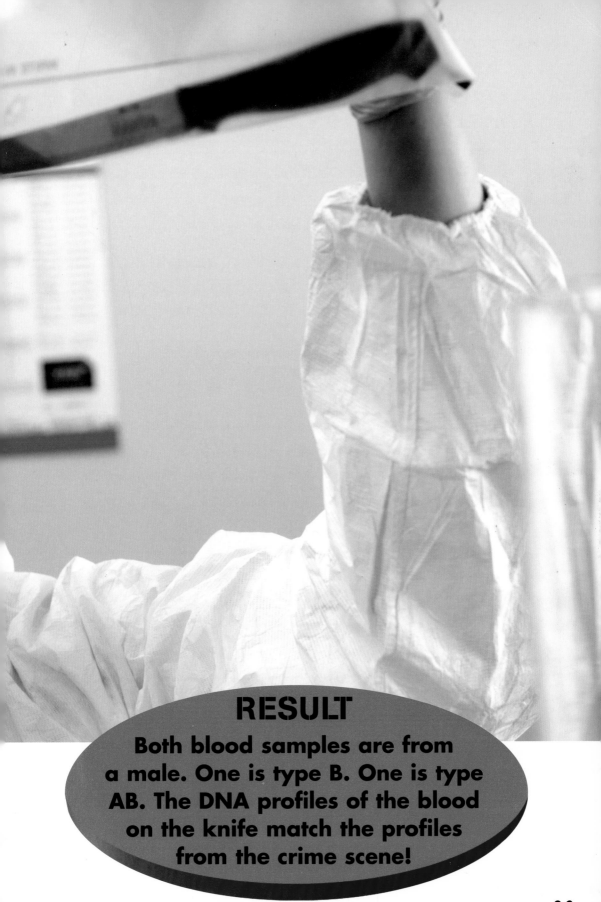

RESULT

Both blood samples are from a male. One is type B. One is type AB. The DNA profiles of the blood on the knife match the profiles from the crime scene!

CHAPTER 4

A BREAKTHROUGH

The ex-girlfriend is the number one suspect.

She had a **motive**. She was angry about the break-up. A knife covered in human blood was found in her garden.

Police diver

The ex-girlfriend says she is **innocent**. She says the knife was planted by the roommate. She says the roommate is trying to **frame** her. The police need more evidence.

Then there is a breakthrough!

A diver finds a man's body in a lake.
Police divers recover the body from the lake.

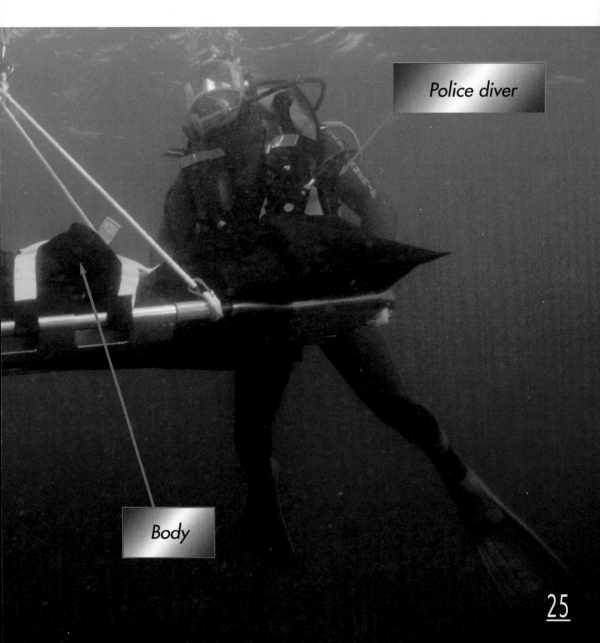

Police diver

Body

The man's body is taken to the crime lab.
There are stab wounds on the body.
It is the missing man!

The man's body was floating face down in the
lake. The body was held down with heavy stones.
But, there is blood **clotted** on the man's back.

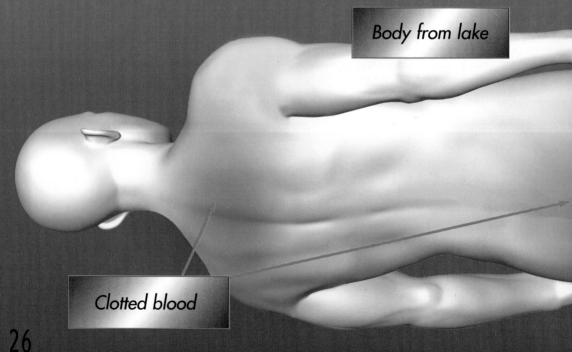

Body from lake

Clotted blood

Blood stops flowing when the heart stops beating. **Gravity** pulls blood to the body parts closest to the ground. The blood clots and stays there.

Could this mean that the man was on his back when he died?

Was his body then moved to the lake?

This blood evidence can sometimes help the police piece together what happened in a murder case.

A forensic scientist runs blood tests on the body.

RESULT

The man's blood is type AB. His DNA profile matches the blood samples from the bathtub and the knife.

CHAPTER 5

THE CHARGE

The police think the man was stabbed in his apartment. Then his body was dumped in the lake. But who committed the crime?

The ex-girlfriend

The police question the ex-girlfriend again. She breaks down and tells police what happened.

She says the roommate committed the crime and she helped him. But then the roommate got scared. She says he hid the knife in her garden to frame her.

She says the roommate cut himself with the knife during the attack.

The roommate

The police find and arrest the roommate.

The roommate says he is innocent.
He says the ex-girlfriend hates
him and is trying to frame him.

He says he was out of town
when the man was killed.
He has never seen the knife.

A forensic scientist tests the
roommate's blood and makes
a DNA profile.

RESULT

**The roommate's blood is type B.
His DNA profile matches blood
found on the knife and on the
tissue from the crime scene.**

The ex-girlfriend and the roommate
are both charged with murder.

CASE SOLVED!

NEED-TO-KNOW WORDS

analyze Taking something apart to find out what it is made of

cell The smallest living unit of a plant or animal. Body tissue and organs are made up of many cells

chromosome A structure in the nucleus of cells that carries DNA

clot To thicken from a liquid into a solid

crime lab A laboratory with equipment that is used for scientific experiments and tests on crime scene evidence

crime scene Any place where a crime has happened. A crime scene can be a house, a car, or even a field

crime scene investigator (CSI) A person who examines crime scenes and collects evidence

DNA The special code in the center (or nucleus) of each person's cells. Our DNA makes us all unique

evidence Facts and signs that can show what happened during a crime

fingerprint powder A powder used by CSIs and forensic scientists to make fingerprints turn a color so they can be seen

forensic scientist An expert who analyzes evidence from a crime scene

frame To make a false accusation so that an innocent person looks guilty

gravity A force that pulls everything down toward the ground

innocent Free from guilt or blame

motive A reason for committing a crime

nucleus The center part of a cell that contains the DNA

suspect A person who is thought to have committed a crime

swab A piece of equipment used to collect liquids at crime scenes. A swab has a small stick with a cotton tip at one end

test tube A clear, glass tube used in laboratory experiments

victim A person who is hurt or killed from a crime

NEED-TO-KNOW FACTS

- **Collecting DNA**
  DNA can be collected from blood, skin, hair, and nails. It can even be collected from sweat and spit.

- **Blood fact**
  Most adults have about 10 pints (4.7 liters) of blood in their bodies.

- **Blood transfusions**
  Today, many adults donate (give) blood. It is stored in bags in hospitals. If a person loses blood, it can be replaced by donated blood in a blood transfusion.

- **Blood types fact**
  In 1901, a scientist named Karl Landsteiner discovered the four blood types. He named the types A, B, AB, and O. Landsteiner's discovery was important because it helped doctors perform blood transfusions. Blood from a donor needs to match the blood type of the person receiving it.

CRIME ONLINE

www.pbs.org/wnet/redgold/journey/index.html
Find out what blood does inside your body

www.fbi.gov/kids/6th12th/6th12th.htm
How the FBI investigates crimes

www.howstuffworks.com/csi5.htm
All about the world of CSI

Publisher's note to educators and parents:
Our editors have carefully reviewed these websites to ensure that they are suitable for children. Many websites change frequently, however, and we cannot guarantee that a site's future contents will continue to meet our high standards of quality and educational value. Be advised that children should be closely supervised whenever they access the Internet.

INDEX

Printed in the U.S.A. - BG